Button Jewelry
&Accessories

22 Unique Projects

Tair Parnes

Creative Publishing international
Chanhassen, MN

Creative Publishing
international

First published in 2006 by
Creative Publishing international, Inc.
18705 Lake Drive East
Chanhassen, Minnesota 55317
1-800-328-3895
www.creativepub.com
All rights reserved

President/CEO: Ken Fund
Executive Editor: Alison Brown Cerier
Executive Managing Editor: Barbara Harold
Senior Editor: Linda Neubauer
Creative Director: Brad Springer
Production Manager: Linda Halls
Design: Eddie Goldfine
Photography: Catriel Lev and Shoshana Brickman
Layout: Gala Pre Press Ltd.

Printed in China
10 9 8 7 6 5 4 3 2

Library of Congress Cataloging-in-Publication Data

Parnes, Tair.
  Button jewelry & accessories : 20 unique projects / Tair Parnes.
    p. cm.
ISBN-13: 978-1-58923-277-8 (soft cover)
  ISBN-10: 1-58923-277-1 (soft cover)
  1. Button craft. 2. Jewelry making. 3. Handicraft. I. Title. II.
Title: Button jewelry and accessories.
  TT880.P37 2006
  745.594'2--dc2   2006011014

Contents

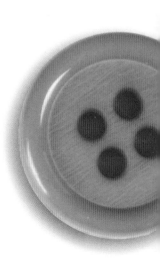

Introduction

Buttons come in almost any shape, color, and size you can imagine. There are two-hole varieties and four-hole types. They may be circular or square, rounded or flat, subtle or bold. There are staid buttons for doing up dress shirts, whimsical ones for closing kids' overalls, and elegant styles for securing wedding gowns and tuxedo jackets.

Buttons may be made from shell, pearl, plastic, or wood. They may also be metallic, enamel, stone, or ceramic. Some buttons are so discreet you barely notice them; others are undeniably audacious. They seem to shout, "See me!" "Look at me!" "I am more than just a fastener. I am a fashion statement!"

With all these distinctions, surely buttons can be used for more than just buttoning!

Buttons are great for accessorizing and enhancing, for adding color, style, and flair. Add buttons to a cotton or leather strap for an eclectic belt; dangle them off jump rings for a one-of-a-kind pair of earrings. Putting beads and buttons together is a simply unbeatable combination that offers endless possibilities.

With *Button Jewelry and Accessories*, you'll learn how to integrate buttons of every shape, size, and color into pieces of jewelry, fashion accessories, and home accents. From handbags and bracelets to sandals and lampshades, you'll discover how to use ordinary (and not-so-ordinary) buttons to create extraordinary pieces of art.

About the Author

Tair Parnes is one of Tel Aviv's most exciting fashion designers. Inspired by vibrant colors and international influences, she excels at taking everyday items and turning them into remarkable objects of art.

Tair has studied a wide range of art forms, from classic art and curatorship to weaving and working with gold. In addition to designing clothing, tapestries, and jewelry, Tair instructs people of all ages in the field of art appreciation, and teaches occupational therapy.

In *Button Jewelry and Accessories*, Tair applies her imagination to one of the world's most common closing devices. She is the artist for whom buttons (and button-lovers) have been waiting!

Tools, Materials, and Basic Techniques

Beading needles

The tools and materials used in these projects can be found in bead shops, sewing stores, and general craft stores. The internet is also an excellent source for ordering materials, especially if you live in an area that doesn't have many craft stores.

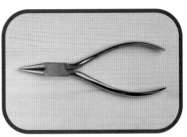

Round-nose pliers

Flat-nose pliers

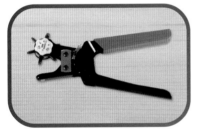

Punch pliers

Scissors

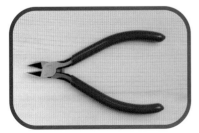

Wire cutters

Tools

Beading needles are necessary for most of the projects in this book. They have very small eyes, allowing you to string seed beads or buttons with very small holes. Beading needles are sized by number: the higher the number, the thinner the needle. For the projects in this book, you'll probably need size 11 or 12 needles. For projects that use only large beads or buttons, you can get away with using regular needles.

Compasses are helpful for drawing accurate circles. If you don't have a compass on hand, you can substitute with a cup, mug, or coaster.

Flat-nose pliers have a flat end and often come with padded handles. They are excellent for opening and closing jump rings, and to hold open jump rings steady while inserting them into button holes.

Punch pliers are used for punching holes in fabric or leather. Most punch pliers allow you to make holes in various sizes. Be sure to select the size of the hole according to the prong in your belt buckle.

Round-nose pliers are aptly named for their round end. They are used to make loops in the end of memory wire, and are helpful for opening and closing jump rings.

Scissors are used to cut string, denim, felt, and paper. Do not use scissors to cut wire, as this will wear down the blades.

Wire cutters are used to cut wire. The thicker the wire, the sturdier your cutters should be.

Wire saws are small saws used to cut delicate metal wire. You don't need one to complete any of the projects in this book, but you will need one if you choose to make your own open jump rings (page 8).

Materials

Beading thread is durable thread, often made from nylon or silk. Unlike sewing thread, it is very strong, and doesn't tear or stretch. Beading thread comes in various widths—when working with seed beads, be sure to select a thread that is very thin. Beading thread also comes in various colors. Because it is usually visible in the finished piece, be sure to choose a color that complements your design.

Beads are available in a vast array of colors, shapes, sizes, and materials. The projects in this book use the beads described below, but feel free to use any beads you like.

Beading thread

Gemstone beads are made from semi-precious stones such as quartz, lapis, and agate. They come in numerous styles, including chip, mini-chip, faceted, and round. Gemstone beads are often sold by the strand.

Glass beads come in vibrant colors, diverse shapes, and a wide range of sizes. Glass beads are often sold in assorted packages, giving you a maximum selection of styles.

Pearl beads are delicate beads made from freshwater or cultured pearls. Glass pearl beads are similar to real pearl beads, and considerably less expensive. Pearl beads come in a variety of shades, and may be smooth or textured. They come in a variety of shapes, and add an elegant touch to any piece of jewelry.

Seed beads are small round beads that come in a wide variety of colors and finishes. They are sized by aughts (rather than inches or millimeters): the higher the number, the smaller the bead. The projects in this book use size 11 beads and size 8 beads. Seed beads are often sold by weight—the quantity of beads per unit varies according to the size and brand.

Seed beads

Buttons are available in an endless variety of colors, shapes, sizes, and materials. Craft stores and sewing shops are excellent starting points for finding buttons, but don't limit yourself to these options. You'll be surprised at how many wonderful buttons you see almost anywhere you look. You may have a stash of loose buttons hidden away in a drawer or sewing kit—don't forget to check out vintage jackets and coats that might be hanging in your closet. There are also great buttons to be found at garage sales, flea markets, and second-hand clothing stores.

The projects in this book use the buttons described below, but don't let yourself be limited! Use whatever buttons catch your eye, tickle your fancy, and make you smile.

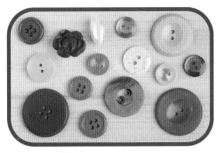

Plastic buttons

Shank buttons

Shell buttons

Plastic buttons come in a wide variety of bright colors. They may be round or square, flat or textured. Plastic buttons are also available in fun shapes such as hearts, flowers, letters, or symbols.

Shank buttons are buttons with a threading hole in the back. They may be made from plastic, glass, wood, or metal.

Shell buttons are elegant and distinct. They may be made from white or colored shell, and come in a variety of shapes and sizes. Some shell buttons are delicately carved, adding a particularly elegant look to any project.

Flax twine is a cord made from linseed, the same material used to make linen. Traditionally used to wrap brown paper packages, flax twine is sold at many art supply stores.

Flexible metal wire is used to make open jump rings (page 8). Any gage of wire is fine, as long as it is stiff enough to hold the shape of the ring. I general use 20 or 24 gage (0.9 mm or 0.6 mm) wire.

Floss elastic cord is great for making bracelets or necklaces that don't require a clasp. It comes in a variety of widths, so be sure to choose one that is thin enough to fit into your smallest bead or button hole.

Jewelry findings are the metal items that finish off a piece of jewelry. They may be made from stainless steel, pewter, sterling silver, or gold. Always choose high quality findings, as you don't want them to rust or break while you are wearing your jewelry.

Barrettes come in various lengths and widths. You can buy them at craft stores, bead stores, and accessory shops.

Clasps are those things we fiddle with when putting on and taking off necklaces and bracelets. The projects in this book use lobster claw clasps, but you can choose any clasp that complements your design (and is easy to open and close!).

Crimps are small metal tubes that are used to hold beads and other material in place. For instructions on how to use crimps, see page 8.

Ear wires turn small (or not so small) beaded masterpieces into dangling earrings. Small hoop earrings can also be used as a base for earrings.

Headpins are straight pins with a flat base at one end. For instructions on how to make dangling beads with headpins, see page 8.

Clasps

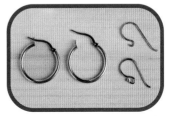

Ear wires

Jump rings

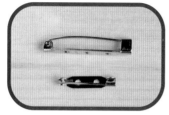

Pin backs

Jump rings are small connector rings that can be pried open and pressed closed. They come in various sizes—be sure to choose the size that is right for your project. When purchasing rings for these projects, be sure to select open rings rather than ones that have been soldered close. Some projects require particularly large jump rings—these may be hard to find, and can be expensive. To make your own jump rings, see below.

Pin backs are used for making pendants and brooches.

Ring bases are usually made from sterling silver or stainless steel. *Charm ring bases* have a protruding hoop or hole; *flat ring bases* have a flat surface. Both types of bases can be found in jewelry supply shop and bead stores.

Lampshade frames come in various sizes, shapes, and styles. They can be found in craft stores, as well as lighting and home decorating stores.

Memory wire is a flexible wire that retains its round shape, and conforms to a certain size after it has been worn a few times. It comes in various sizes, suitable for bracelets, necklaces, and rings.

Sconces are lamp fixtures suited to installation on a wall. Find plain or decorated sconces at craft stores, as well as lighting and home decorating stores.

Silicone cord has a smooth texture and distinct shiny look. It comes in a variety of vibrant colors and various widths. Be sure to choose a width that it is thin enough to fit through your smallest bead or button hole.

Sketching supplies are useful for drawing your design out in advance. Basic items to have on hand include white paper, pencil, eraser, ruler, and marker.

Super glue is used to reinforce knots, and hold beads and buttons in place. The type sold in hardware stores is fine for these projects, although you can also find a large variety of appropriate adhesives at any bead stores. Be sure to choose glue this is quick-drying and water resistant. Make sure the variety you select comes in a jar with a fine spout, for precisely applying the glue.

Basic Techniques

Flattening crimps

Crimps are small metal tubes that are made to be flattened. They can be used to attach two ends of string together, or to hold beads in place. To flatten a crimp, simply hold the crimp in place with a pair of flat-nose pliers and gently press the sides together.

Making dangling beads

To turn a regular bead into a dangling bead, insert a headpin into the bead, and slide the bead down so it rests on the flat end of headpin. Using round-nose pliers, twist the top of the headpin into a loop. Cut off any excess wire with wire cutters.

Making open jump rings

Several projects in this book call for open jump rings, sometimes as many as 200 or more! Making your own jump rings is easy, and can be much less expensive than buying prepared ones. You'll need flexible metal wire to make the rings—I usually use 20 or 24 gauge (0.9 mm or 0.6 mm) wire, but any wire that is flexible enough to wrap will do. You'll also need a wooden dowel in the appropriate diameter, and a wire saw.

Wrap the wire around the dowel in a tight coil. Make as many rounds as you need jump rings. When the wire is tightly coiled, use the saw to cut the wire in a straight line along the length of the dowel.

Opening and closing jump rings

The easiest way to open and close jump rings is by using two sets of pliers. Two flat-nose pliers are best, but you can use round-nose pliers as well. If you have only one set of pliers, that's fine too; you'll just have to grasp one end of the jump ring with your fingers.

To open the ring, hold one set of pliers in each hand and grasp one end of the jump ring in each set of pliers. Position the ring so that you see through the hole. Now draw one pair of pliers towards you and push the other pair away. **Do not unroll the jump ring.** To close the ring, draw the pliers back to their original position.

Sewing buttons together

To sew two 2-hole buttons together, hold the buttons so they are back to back, with the holes lined up. Insert the thread into the bottom hole of one button, and out the corresponding hole of the other button. Draw the thread through, leaving a 2" (5 cm) tail behind the first button. Insert the thread into the top hole of the second button, and out the corresponding hole of the first button. Repeat the process to secure the buttons. Tie a knot with the tail thread and cut both ends close to the knot. The technique for sewing 4-hole buttons together is almost identical, just insert the thread on a diagonal each time you insert it into the same button, and repeat the process twice, to make an X on each button.

Sewing buttons onto fabric

To sew a 2-hole button onto fabric, insert the thread on the underside of the fabric and draw out through the top. Draw the thread out a button hole, leaving a 2" (5 cm) tail on the underside of the fabric. Insert the thread into an empty hole and draw through to the underside of the fabric. Tie a knot with the tail to secure. The technique for sewing a 4-hole button onto fabric is almost identical, just insert the thread on a diagonal each time you insert it into the same button, and repeat the process twice, to make an X on each button.

Keep in Mind

Making jewelry and accessories with your own two hands is fun and rewarding—it's also a great way to wind down after a busy day, or to relax on weekends and holidays. Here are some points to keep in mind as you work:

Follow your instinct

Feel free to alter any project in this book by using different colors or sizes of buttons and beads. You can even make the same project several times using different materials—you'll be surprised at how different the results will be!

Length of thread

I generally work with very long pieces of thread, because I find them easier to handle. It also means I won't run out of thread before my project is finished. If you find it more comfortable working with shorter thread, go right ahead.

Planning a pattern

Everybody has their own work style. Some people like to plan their pattern in advance; others like to improvize as they go. Play around with the buttons before you start, and choose the method that comes naturally to you.

Quantities

All of the quantities in this book are based on the sizes of the beads and buttons I used. The materials you use will likely be somewhat different, so be sure to adjust the quantities of your materials accordingly. I suggest overestimating when buying materials for a specific project—it's better to have leftovers at the end, rather than running out along the way!

Sizes

All of the sizes are flexible. If you want longer earrings, a shorter necklace, or a wider belt, that's fine—just remember to adjust your materials accordingly.

Jewelry

Cappuccino Cream Necklace

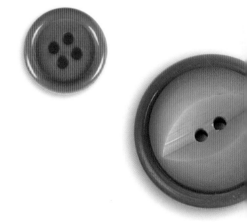

This necklace uses a combination of colored pearl beads and white shell buttons. A sprinkling of red seed beads adds a dash of cinnamon, completing the look. This design is particularly long, producing a 6½' (2 m) necklace that fits loosely around the neck three times.

Materials

18 pairs white 2-hole shell buttons, ½" to 1" (1.3 cm to 2.5 cm) in diameter, various shapes
162 pearl beads, ¼" to ½" (0.6 cm to 1.3 cm) in diameter, various colors
180 seed beads, size 11, red
Beading thread
Super glue

Beading needle
Scissors

Directions

 Thread the needle with 19½' (6 m) beading thread. Double the thread and tie the ends together, leaving a 2" (5 cm) tail after the knot. String 9 to 11 pearl beads.

 Hold a pair of buttons together back to back, with their holes lined up. Insert the thread into the bottom hole of one button and out the corresponding hole of the other button. Insert the thread into the top hole of the second button, and out the corresponding hole of the first button.

 Gently pull the thread taut, making sure the buttons are snug against each other, and flush against the pearl beads. Draw the thread out the bottom hole of one button and string 4 to 5 seed beads. Insert the thread into the other hole of that button, and out the corresponding hole of the other button.

 String 4 to 5 seed beads and insert the thread into the other hole of that button.

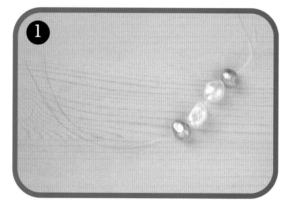

14

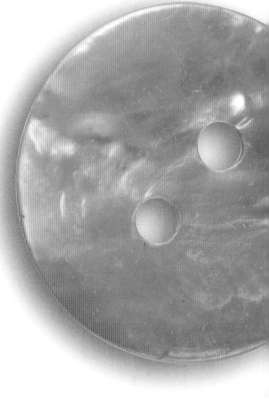

 5 Draw the thread out from between the two buttons, and gently pull taut so that the seed beads lay flat against the buttons.

 6 String 9 to 11 pearl beads.

7 Repeat steps 2 to 6 until the necklace is the right length, taking care to finish with a pair of buttons.

8 Tie a knot after the last pair of buttons, then tie the ends of the necklace together. Reinforce with a drop of glue, and cut the thread close to the knot.

OPTION
I used freshwater pearls in this design, but you can substitute with glass or cultured pearl beads. Less expensive than freshwater varieties, these beads will still produce an elegant and impressive pearly necklace.

Eye Candy Necklace

This colorful glass bead and button necklace is sweeter than sugar—and much better for your teeth. The length is about 42" (107 cm), and it wraps loosely around the neck a couple of times.

Materials

11 pairs shell buttons, ½" to 1" (1.3 cm to 2.5 cm) in diameter, various shapes and styles
200 glass beads, various shapes, sizes, and colors
110 seed beads, size 11, various colors
Beading thread
Super glue

Beading needle
Scissors

Directions

1 Thread the needle with 10½' (3.2 m) of beading thread. Double the thread and tie the ends together, leaving a 2" (5 cm) tail after the knot.

2 String a seed bead to act as a stopper and prevent the larger beads from falling off the thread. Loop the thread around the bead and draw it through again to secure the bead in place.

3 String 12 to 20 glass beads, in various shapes, sizes, and colors.

18

4 Hold a pair of buttons together back to back, with their holes lined up. If they are 2-hole buttons, insert the thread into the bottom hole of one button and out the corresponding hole of the other button. Insert the thread into the top hole of the second button, and out the corresponding hole of the first button. If they are 4-hole buttons, insert the thread on a diagonal each time, and repeat to make an X on each side of the buttons.

 5 Gently pull the thread taut, making sure the buttons are snug against each other, and flush against the glass beads. If they are 2-hole buttons, draw the thread out the bottom hole of one button and string 4 to 5 seed beads. Insert the thread into the other hole of that button, and out the corresponding hole of the other button. String 4 to 5 seed beads and insert the thread into the other hole of that button. If they are 4-hole buttons, insert the thread on a diagonal each time, and repeat to make an X on each side of the buttons.

 6 Draw the thread out from between the two buttons, and pull gently so that the seed beads lay flat against the buttons.

 7 String 12 to 20 glass beads.

8 Repeat steps 3 to 7 until the necklace is the right length, taking care to finish with a pair of buttons.

9 Tie a knot after the last pair of buttons, then tie the ends of the necklace together. Reinforce with a drop of glue, and cut the thread close to the knot.

OPTION
There is no need to be consistent in the number or types of glass beads you string between each pair of buttons—variety is part of this necklace's charm! Feel free to incorporate any funky beads you have, or leftover beads from another project.

Elemental Elegance Necklace

Metallic rings bring a modern simplicity to this design. Choose buttons with a shiny finish for a totally modern look, or use soft shades for contrast.

Materials

65 pairs shell buttons, various shapes, styles, and colors
65 open jump rings, ½" (1.3 cm) in diameter

Flat-nose pliers
Round-nose pliers

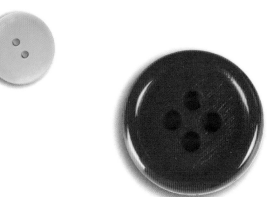

Directions

1 Hold a pair of buttons back to back, so that the holes are lined up. Using the pliers, open a jump ring (page 8) and insert one end through corresponding holes in the buttons.

2 Hold another pair of buttons back to back and insert the same jump ring into corresponding holes. Close the jump ring.

3 Open another jump ring and insert one end through the empty holes in the second pair of buttons. If these are 4-hole buttons, choose the holes that are on a diagonal to the holes holding the first jump ring.

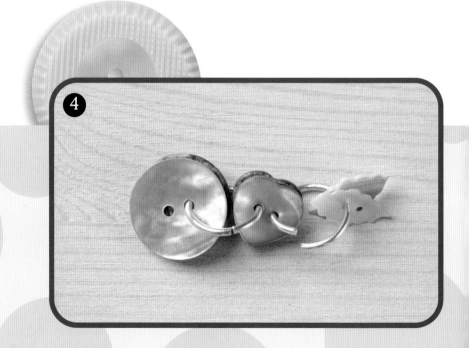

4 Hold another pair of buttons back to back and string onto the open jump ring. Close the jump ring. Now you should have three pairs of buttons held together with two jump rings.

5 Repeat steps 3 and 4 until the necklace is the right length.

6 To close the necklace, open a jump ring and insert one end through the empty hole in first pair of buttons. Insert the other end in the empty hole in the last pair of buttons and close.

OPTION
The size of the jump rings you need for this necklace depends upon the size of your buttons. If you are using particularly large buttons, you'll need large jump rings, too. For instructions on how to make your own jump rings, see page 8.

Cloud Nine Necklace

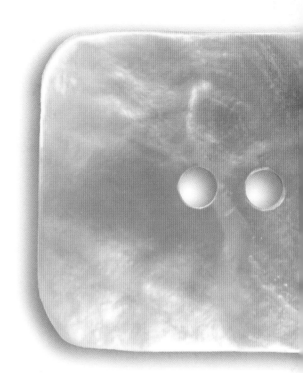

This necklace is bubbly, bold, and beautiful. Use red cord for a vivid look, blue cord for a dreamy look, or black cord for a modern look.

Materials

89 round white 2-hole buttons, 1/2" (1.3 cm) in diameter
Silicone cord, red, 0.04" (0.1 cm) in diameter
85 crimps, 1/4" (0.6 cm) in length
Super glue

Scissors
Flat-nose pliers
Wire cutters

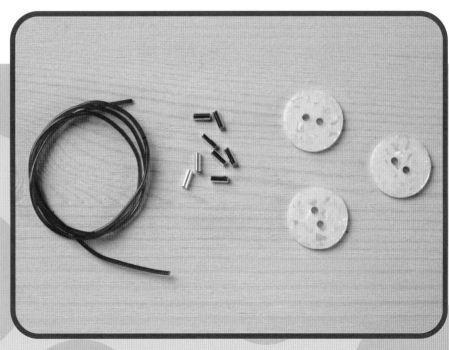

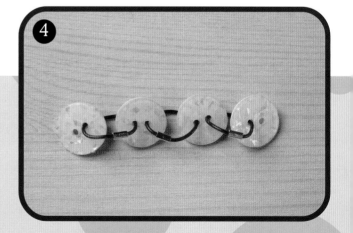

Directions

1 Cut the cord into 100 pieces, each 1½" (3.8 cm) long.

2 Draw the left end of a piece of cord through the right hole of a button. Draw the right end of the cord through the left hole of another button. Work patiently, because the cord is short and may slip out of the holes.

3 Insert each end of the cord into either end of a crimp. Flatten the crimp (page 8), securing the ends of the cord inside. Add a drop of glue to secure the cord inside the crimp.

4 Draw the left end of a piece of cord through the empty hole of the button on the right. Draw the right end of the cord through the left hole of another button. Repeat step 3 to connect. Continue in this manner to create a chain of buttons.

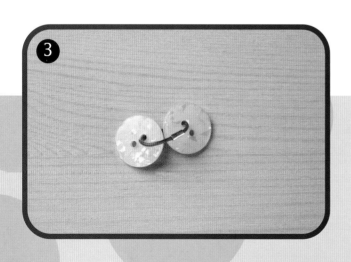

In total, you'll need to make five chains of buttons, in the following lengths: A—12 buttons, B—13 buttons, C—16 buttons, D—19 buttons, E—20 buttons.

Attach chains A and B by drawing a piece of cord through the empty left holes in the leftmost buttons on each chain, and through the right hole of another button. Draw the ends of the cord together and insert into a crimp. Flatten the crimp, adding a drop of glue to secure.

Attach chains A and B at the other end as well, using the technique described in step 6.

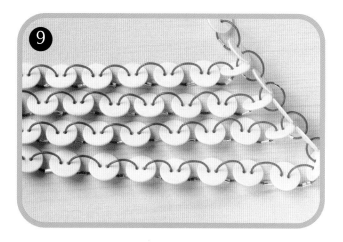

Attach chain ABC to chain D; then attach chain ABCD to chain E.

Now attach chain AB to chain C in a similar manner, by drawing a piece of cord through the empty left holes in the buttons on the left of chain AB and chain C, and through the right hole of another button. Flatten a crimp over the ends, adding a drop of glue to secure. Repeat at the other end using the same technique.

To make the clasp, draw a piece of cord through both holes of the last button on the left end of the necklace. Form a loop by flattening a crimp over the ends. Unlike other loops you have made until now, this loop runs through both holes in a single button.

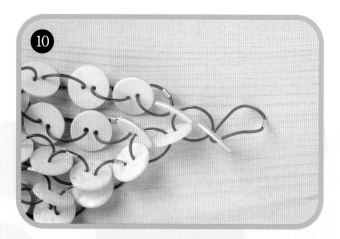

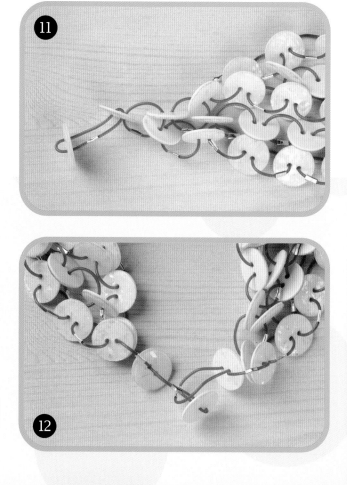

Now draw a piece of cord through both holes of the last button on the right end of the necklace. Draw the cord through both holes in another button. Flatten a crimp over the ends, adding a drop of glue to secure.

To fasten the necklace, draw the button attached in step 11 through the loop you made in step 12.

OPTION
Make this necklace thicker or thinner by increasing or decreasing the number of chains. Just make sure that each chain has a different number of buttons, and always increase the number of buttons in the chains gradually.

Sheerly Shell Necklace

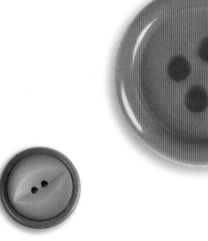

Anyone who loves the seashore will enjoy wearing this shell necklace. It's perfect for dressing up a summer frock, or adding a breath of fresh sea air to a business outfit. Using twine completes the natural look, but any rugged string can be used instead.

Materials

19 shell buttons, 1" to 1¾" (2.5 cm to 4.4 cm) in diameter, various shapes and colors
Flax twine, unbleached
Super glue

Scissors

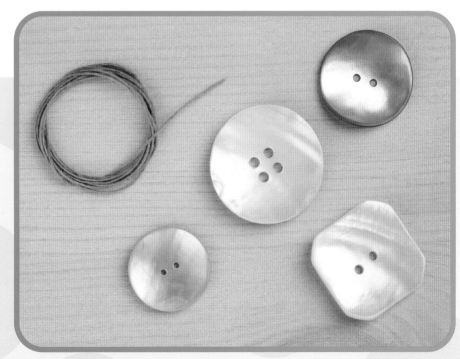

Directions

 Cut an 8' (2.4 m) piece of twine, and fold it near the middle, so that one strand is about 2' (61 cm) longer than the other.

 Tie a slip knot near the fold, forming a loop that is slightly larger than the smallest button. This loop will form half of the clasp. Set aside the smallest button for the clasp—you'll need it in step 8.

 Buttonhole-knot the longer strand around the loop in the following manner. Insert the longer strand into the loop from behind. Draw out the front, and insert into the loop in the longer strand. Pull gently to secure. Repeat to make continuous buttonhole knots along the entire loop. Now you should have two strands of twine, of almost equal length, extending from the loop.

 String a button onto one strand by drawing the twine over the top of the button and inserting it downward through the first hole. Draw the other strand under the button and insert it upward through the second hole.

 Slide the button along until it is flush against the loop. Tie the two strands together immediately after the button to secure it in place.

 String another button onto the twine following the technique described in step 4. Slide the button until it is flush against the previous button and tie the two strands together immediately after the button.

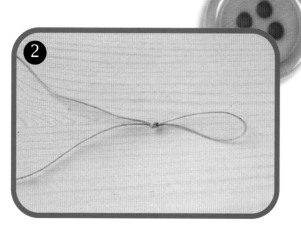

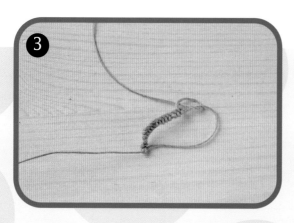

Repeat step 6 to string all of the buttons, except the smallest one, onto the twine.

Tie a double knot after the last button and secure with a drop of glue. Cut off one of the strands close to the knot.

To make the clasp, insert the remaining strand through one hole in the smallest button and out the other hole. Slide the button along until it is about 1" (2.5 cm) from the last button in the necklace. Tie a knot in the twine to secure the button in place.

Buttonhole-knot the strand around the length of twine between the clasp button and the last button in the necklace. Tie a knot when you reach the last button in the necklace, secure with a drop of glue, and trim any remaining twine.

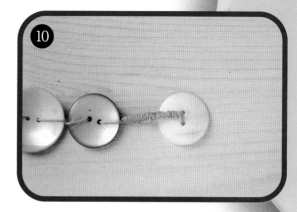

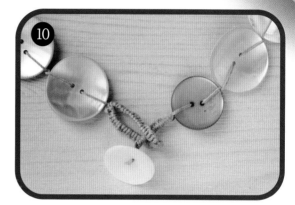

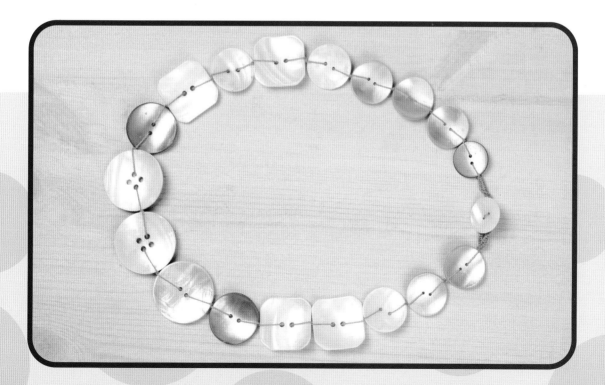

33

Starry Night Necklace and Bracelet Set

This dazzling ensemble features hundreds of sparkling quartz beads and a variety of glass and rhinestone shank buttons. If you have trouble finding dangling quartz beads, you can make them yourself by stringing each bead onto a headpin (page 7), though this does take a lot of time.

Materials

600 to 800 dangling quartz mini-chip beads
100 to 120 shank buttons, various shapes and styles
Floss elastic cord, white, 0.5 mm in diameter
Super glue

Scissors

Directions

1 To make a bracelet, unwind some elastic cord, but do not cut.

2 String 6 to 14 beads, then string a button.

3 Continue stringing beads and buttons onto the cord. There is no need to be consistent in the number of beads or types of buttons you string. Make sure the beads and buttons lie flush against each other, so the bracelet has a dense, full look.

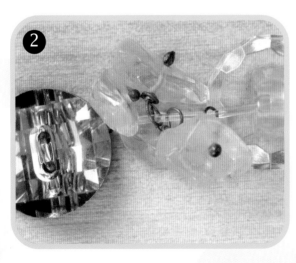

4 Measure the bracelet against your wrist as you work. Each bracelet in this set measures 6" (15 cm), and has about 100 beads and 16 buttons. When your bracelet is the right length, tie a double knot in the cord and secure with a drop of glue. Cut the cord close to the knot.

5 To make a necklace, unwind some elastic cord, but do not cut. Follow steps 2 and 3, stringing beads and buttons until the necklace is long enough to fit comfortably over your neck. The necklace measures 30" (76 cm), and has about 500 beads and 80 buttons. When the necklace is the right length for you, tie a double knot in the cord and secure with a drop of glue. Cut the cord close to the knot.

Bubblegum Bracelet

Using bright pink buttons give this bracelet a playful look. Try black buttons for a more sophisticated style, or assorted colors to create something funky and fun.

Materials

30 pink 4-hole buttons, ¾" (1.9 cm) in diameter
44 open jump rings, ½" (1.3 cm) in diameter
2 open jump rings, ¼" (0.6 cm) in diameter
Lobster claw clasp

Flat-nose pliers
Round-nose pliers

Directions

 Using the pliers, open two large jump rings (page 9). Note that you'll be using only large jump rings until step 14. Insert both rings into the same hole in a button.

 Insert each ring into a hole in another button and close. Now you should have two rings holding three buttons together.

 Attach the two new buttons to each other by inserting a jump ring into adjacent empty holes in the buttons. Gently close the ring. Open a jump ring and insert it into the empty hole on the left of the button on the left. Open another ring and insert it into the empty hole on the right of the button on the right. Do not close the jump rings.

 Insert jump rings into the other empty holes of the buttons added in step 2. Insert these two rings into a single hole in a new button and close.

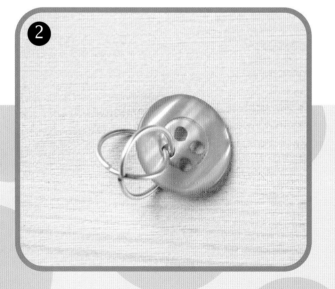

5 Insert two rings into the unused holes on the left and right side of the new button, leaving the bottom hole empty for now. Attach buttons to each of these rings and close the rings.

6 Insert the rings on the far left and far right of two buttons added in step 2 into appropriate hole in the buttons added in step 5. Close the rings. Now you should have a pyramid of six buttons, held together with nine rings.

7 Separately, make a chain of three buttons by opening a jump ring and inserting each end into a new button. Close the jump ring. Open another jump ring and insert one end into the empty right hole in the button on the right. Inset the other end of the jump ring into another button and close.

8 To attach this 3-button chain to the 9-button pyramid completed in step 6, lay the chain along the bottom of the pyramid. Open a jump ring and insert one end into the bottom hole of the leftmost button in the pyramid. Insert the other end of the ring into the top hole of the leftmost button of the chain. Close the ring. Connect the middle and rightmost buttons in the pyramid and the chain in the same manner.

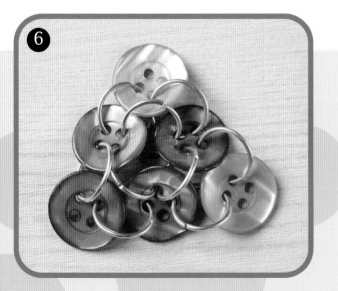

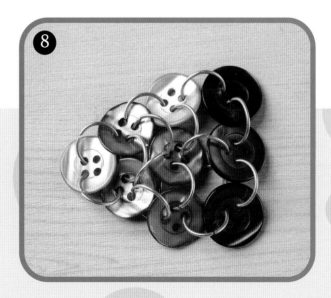

9 Repeat steps 7 and 8 to make more 3-button chains and attach them to the pyramid. This design requires six 3-button chains, but the number of chains your bracelet requires depends upon the size of your wrist. As you work, remember to take into account that ending the bracelet adds about 2" (5 cm) to the length.

10 When you're ready to begin ending the bracelet, open four jump rings. Insert one ring in the bottom hole of each of the three bottom buttons. Insert a second ring in the bottom hold of the middle button.

11 Insert the jump ring from the leftmost button, and one of the rings from the middle button, into a single hole in a new button. Close the ring. Insert the ring from the rightmost button, and the other ring from the middle button, into a single hole in another new button. Close the ring.

Insert a jump ring into the bottom hole in one of the bottom two buttons. Draw the ring into a hole in a new button and close. Insert a second jump ring into the bottom hole of the other bottom button. Draw the ring through the hole with the jump ring in the new button and close.

Attach one of the small jump rings into the bottommost hole of the button at the bottom of the bracelet.

Attach these two buttons together by inserting a jump ring through adjacent holes in the buttons. Close the ring.

Attach the other small jump ring to the topmost hole of the button at the top of the bracelet and attach the clasp.

Tutti Frutti Bracelet

With brightly colored plastic beads, this bracelet looks almost good enough to eat!

Materials

60 round 2-hole buttons, ½" (1.3 cm) in diameter, various colors
30 open jump rings, ¼" (0.6 cm) in diameter
Lobster claw clasp

Flat-nose pliers
Round-nose pliers

Directions

 Using the pliers, open a jump ring (page 9). Insert each end of the ring into a different color button and close the ring.

 Open another jump ring and insert each end into a different color button. Draw the ring through the first jump ring and close. Now you should have two connected jump rings, each of which has two buttons.

4 After attaching the last set of buttons to a jump ring, draw the ring through the last jump ring in the bracelet, but don't close. String the clasp onto the jump ring and close.

3 Repeat step 2, using various colors of buttons, until the bracelet is the right length.

OPTION
Use larger buttons to make a bolder bracelet or smaller buttons for a more delicate look. Be sure to adjust the size of the jump rings according to the size of your buttons. If your buttons are particularly large, you may want to make your own jump rings. See page 8 for instructions.

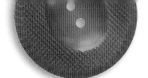

Rosy Red Bracelet

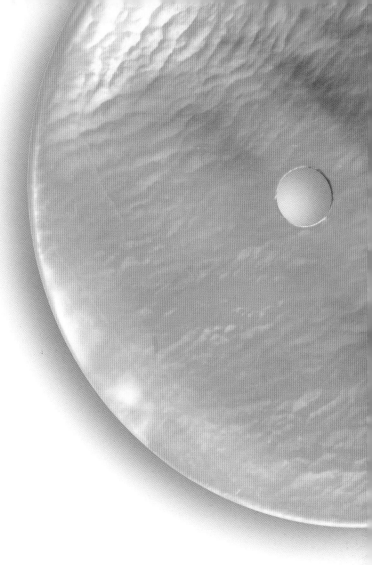

You'll always have a bouquet on hand with this floral bracelet. Using memory wire means you never have to fiddle with a clasp.

Materials

32 red flower shank buttons, ¾" (1.3 cm) in diameter
Bracelet memory wire

Round-nose pliers
Wire cutters

Directions

 Cut 1½ loops of memory wire—measure against your wrist to make sure it is enough. Use the pliers to form a small loop at one end of the wire. This loop prevents the buttons from slipping off, and forms half of the clasp.

 Hold two buttons back to back so that the shanks are flush against each other, and the holes are lined up. String the buttons onto the wire until they reach the loop.

String two more buttons in this manner, orienting them so that they overlap slightly with the first pair of buttons. If your buttons are not symmetrical, be sure to orient all of the buttons in the same direction.

 Repeat step 3 until the bracelet is the right length.

 Use wire cutters to trim the wire 1/2" (0.6 cm) from the last pair of buttons. Use the pliers to form a small loop at this end of the wire. This loop prevents the buttons from sliding off and forms the other half of the clasp. Cut the wire at the end of the loop.

Flower Power Brooch

The flower in this brooch never droops or fades. It doesn't need water either—just vivid felt, bright beads, and a few simple stitches.

Materials

2 pieces red felt, 4" × 4" (10 cm × 10 cm)
Round orange 2-hole button, 1" (2.5 cm) in diameter
350 seed beads, size 11, various colors
Pin back
Beading thread

Compass
Scissors
Beading needle

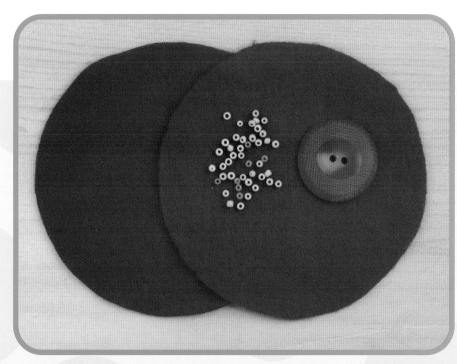

Directions

 Cut each piece of felt into a circle with a 4" (10 cm) diameter. You can use a compass for this, or trace the bottom of a wide mug or cup.

 Thread the needle with a comfortable length of thread, double it and tie both ends together.

 Working with one circle at a time, insert the needle into the middle of the felt. Sew a running stitch to the edge, then back to the center.

 Gently pull the thread taut to form soft wrinkles in the felt. Tie a knot close to the felt to hold the wrinkles in place.

 Working at a 120° angle from the first row of stitches, make another running stitch from the center of the felt to the edge, then back to the center.

3

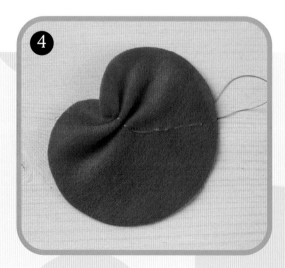

4

6 Gently pull the thread to form soft wrinkles and tie a knot close to the felt to hold the wrinkles in place.

 7 Repeat steps 5 and 6 to make a third line of stitches. At this point, your felt should have the shape of a three-petal flower.

 8 Repeat steps 3 to 7 with the other piece of felt to make another three-petal flower.

9 Place one flower over the other, orienting them so that all six petals are showing. Sew the flowers together at the center.

10 Sew the button onto the front of the flower, at the center.

9

10

11

13

12 Draw the thread out the front of one button hole. String 4 to 5 beads then insert into the other hole. Secure with a stitch in the felt.

11 Repeat step 13 using various colors of beads to make several branches around the button. Tie a double knot after the last branch and cut the thread close to the knot.

13 Draw the thread out from between the button and the flower. String 14 turquoise beads and a yellow bead. Loop the thread around the yellow bead and draw back through 7 turquoise beads. String 7 more turquoise beads and a yellow bead. Loop the thread around the yellow bead and draw back through 7 turquoise beads. Draw the thread through the first 7 turquoise beads that were strung. These beads will be partially concealed under the button.

11 Sew the pin back onto the back of the flower, at the center.

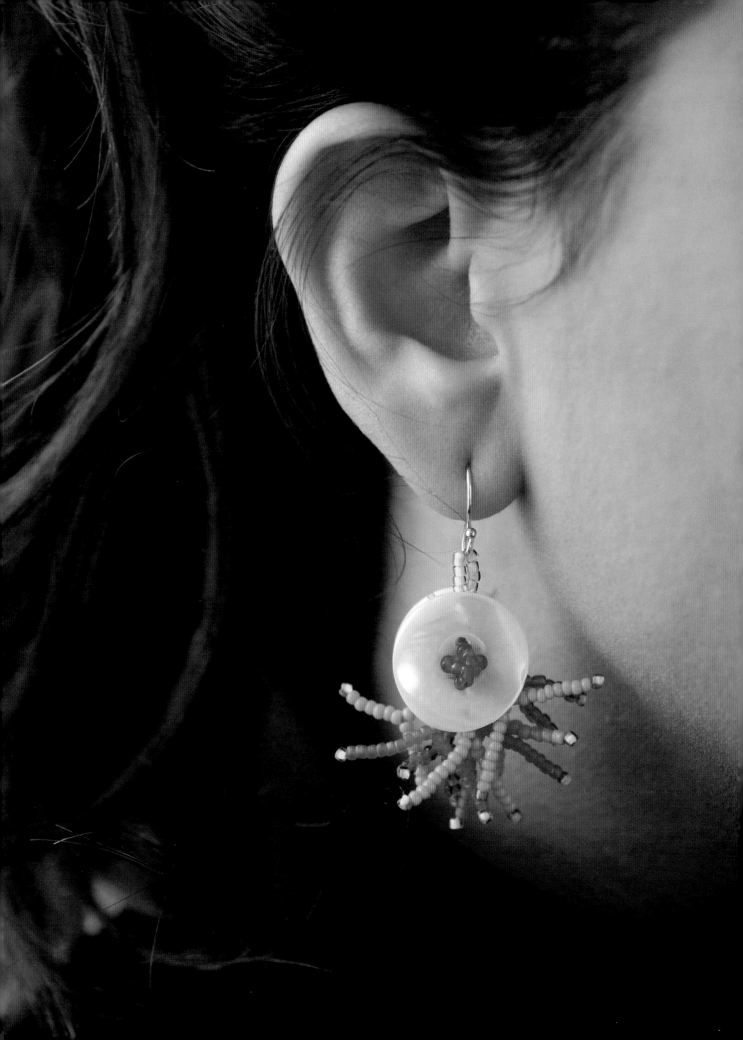

Caribbean Dive Earrings

With bright green, orange, and pink seed beads, these dangling earrings will remind you—and anyone who sees you wearing them—of a magnificent coral reef.

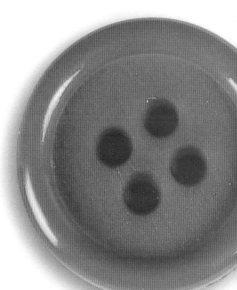

Materials

4 round white 4-hole shell buttons, 1" (2.5 cm) in diameter
460 seed beads, size 11, various colors
Beading thread
Pair of ear wires

Beading needle
Scissors

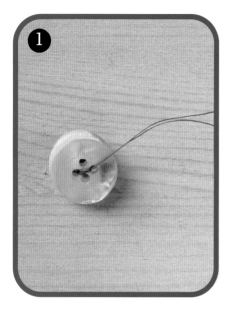

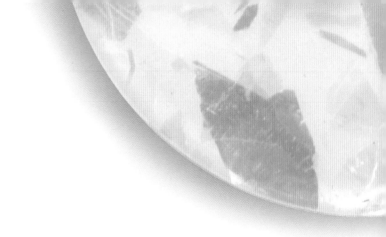

Directions

 Thread the needle with a comfortable length of thread, double it, and sew one pair of buttons together (page 9).

 String 4 to 6 red beads and insert the thread on a diagonal, drawing it through to one of the unused holes in the other button.

 Draw the thread out the front of one button and string 4 to 6 red beads. Insert the thread on a diagonal, drawing it out through the corresponding hole in the other button.

 String 5 to 7 red beads and insert the thread on a diagonal, creating an X of beads. Draw the thread out through the corresponding hole in the other button.

String 5 to 7 red beads and insert the thread on a diagonal, creating an X of beads on this button as well. Pull the thread out from between the two buttons.

 String 15 pink beads and a turquoise bead. Loop the thread around the turquoise bead and draw back through 9 pink beads. String 9 more pink beads and a turquoise bead. Loop the thread around the turquoise bead and draw back through 9 pink beads. Draw the thread back through the first 6 pink beads that were strung. These beads will be partially concealed under the button. Draw the thread through the stitches connecting the two buttons to secure it in place.

 Repeat step 6, using various colors of beads, to make several branches extending from the bottom of the buttons.

 Draw the thread upwards from between the two buttons. String 10 beads and draw the thread back to the middle of the buttons. Wrap the thread around the stitching between the two buttons several times to secure, tie in a double knot, and cut close to the knot.

 Repeat steps 1 to 8 to make the second earring. Attach each earring to an ear wire.

Cinnamon Stick Earrings

Spice up your jewelry box with these dangly button earrings. The beading thread is quite visible in this design, so be sure to select thread and beads that match.

Materials

4 white 4-hole shell buttons, 1" (2.5 cm) in diameter
4 white 4-hole shell buttons, ¾" (1.9 cm) in diameter
4 white 4-hole shell buttons, ½" (1.3 cm) in diameter
36 seed beads, size 8, red
Beading thread, red
Pair of small hoop earrings

Beading needle
Scissors

Directions

1 Thread the needle with a comfortable length of thread, double it, and sew pairs of buttons together (page 9). You will use one pair of buttons in each size for each earring.

2 Draw the thread into the stitching that holds the smallest pair of buttons together and wrap around to secure. Draw the thread through the stitching that holds the medium pair of buttons together and wrap around to secure. Draw the thread through the stitching that holds the largest pair of buttons together and wrap around to secure. Allow the thread to extend upward from between the pair of largest buttons.

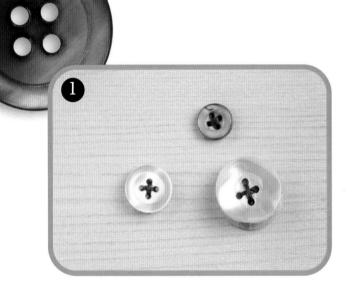

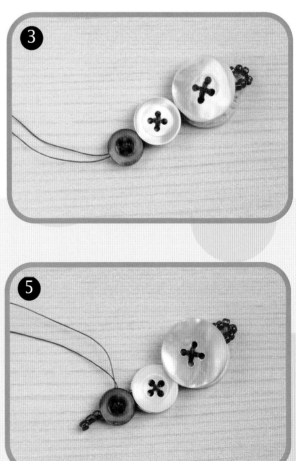

 3 String 9 beads and create a loop by bringing the thread back to the stitching connecting the largest pair of buttons. Draw the thread through the stitching that connects the medium and small pairs of buttons.

 5 Loop the thread around the last bead and draw back through the other 2 beads. Secure by drawing the thread through the stitching holding together this pair of buttons.

 6 Repeat steps 4 and 5 to make two more branches extending from the smallest pair of buttons. Tie the thread in a double knot and cut close to the knot.

 4 Draw the thread out from between the smallest pair of buttons and string 3 beads.

 7 Repeat steps 2 to 6 to make the second earring. Attach the loop at the top of each earring to a hoop earring.

Bundles of Buttons Earrings

Use turquoise, azure, aquamarine, indigo, and sapphire buttons to create vibrantly varied bundles of blue and green buttons.

Materials

42 round 4-hole shell buttons, 1/4" to 1/2" (0.6 cm to 1.3 cm) in diameter, various shades of blue and green
32 open jump rings, 1/4" (0.6 cm) in diameter
Pair of ear wires

Flat-nose pliers
Round-nose pliers

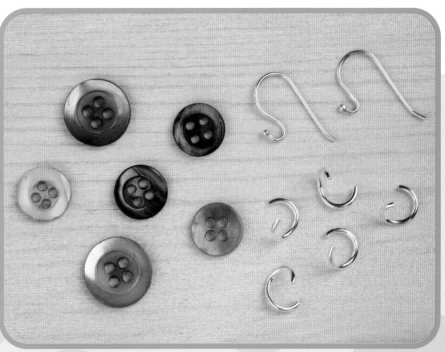

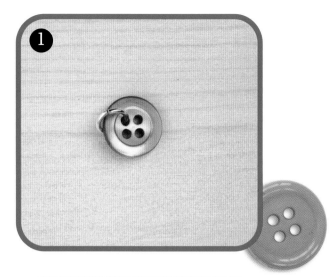

Directions

Using the pliers, open a jump ring (page 9). Insert one end of the ring into a button hole and close the ring.

Open another jump ring and insert each end into a separate button. Draw the ring through the ring attached to the first button and close.

Open another jump ring, attach another button, then draw the open ring through the ring connecting the two buttons. Close the ring.

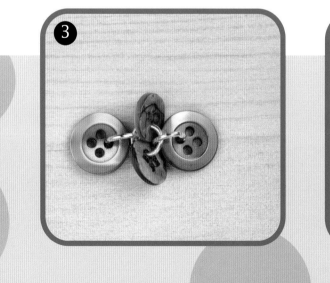

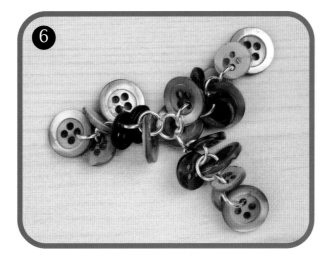

4 Repeat steps 2 to 3 to make a fringe of buttons. Make the fringe as long as you like, and using whatever combination of buttons you like.

6 To make an earring, open a jump ring and string three fringes onto the ring.

5 Repeat steps 1 to 4 to make five more button fringes. If you want symmetrical earrings, be sure to note the length and colors in each fringe, and make pairs of identical fringes.

7 Repeat step 6 to make the second earring. Attach an ear wire to the top ring of each earring.

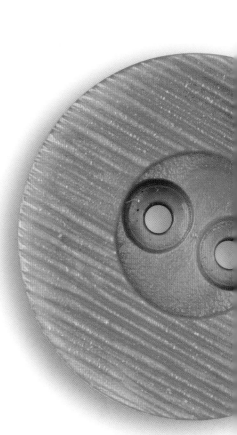

Fantasy Fountain Ring

This metallic ring is bursting with style. Bold yet simple, it won't go unnoticed.

Materials

Round silver 2-hole button, 1¼" (3.2 cm) in diameter
6 oval silver 2-hole buttons, ¼" (0.6 cm) in diameter
Flat ring base with a 1¼" (3.2 cm) base
66 seed beads, size 11, red
Beading thread
Super glue

Beading needle
Scissors

Directions

1 Thread the needle with a comfortable length of thread and double it. There is no need to tie the ends together.

2 Insert the thread in a hole in the large button, draw it over the top of the button and through the other hole. Pull the thread through until there is a 2" (5 cm) tail extending from the back. Tie the thread in a double knot on the underside of the button, securing the thread in place. Do not cut the tail. Draw the thread up through one of the holes in the button.

4

5

6

To make a fountain of beads, string 8 beads onto the thread. Insert the thread through a hole in a small button, string 3 beads, then insert through the other hole in the same button.

 When you have made six fountains of beads, draw the thread out the bottom of the large button and tie in a double knot with the remaining tail. Cut both ends of the thread close to the knot.

 Draw the thread back through the 8 beads and insert into the same hole in the large button. Pull gently to secure, then push the thread out of the other hole.

 Glue the flower onto the ring base. Set aside to dry thoroughly before wearing.

Repeat steps 3 and 4, using alternate holes in the large button for each fountain.

Over-the-Moon Charm Ring

This ring jingles pleasantly whenever you move your hand. Using shiny white shell buttons gives it an elegant, almost moonlike appearance.

Materials

8 white shell shank buttons, 1/2" (1.3 cm) in diameter
Charm ring base
Beading thread
Super glue

Beading needle
Scissors

Directions

 Thread the needle with a comfortable length of thread and double it. There is no need to tie the ends together.

 Insert the thread into the hole in the charm ring and pull through until a 2" (5 cm) tail extends from the other side of the hole. Tie the tail and thread in a double knot around the hole in the ring base.

 Insert the thread into the hole in the charm ring. String a button onto the thread then loop the thread around the hole in the charm ring. Tie a knot around the hole to secure.

 4 String the rest of the buttons in the same manner, gently pulling the thread taut between each button. There is no need to tie a knot after every bead, but you can draw the thread through the holes in buttons that are already attached to secure the buttons in place.

 5 When you have secured all of the buttons, tie the thread and the tail in a double knot and cut close to the knot. Add a drop of glue to secure.

Accessories

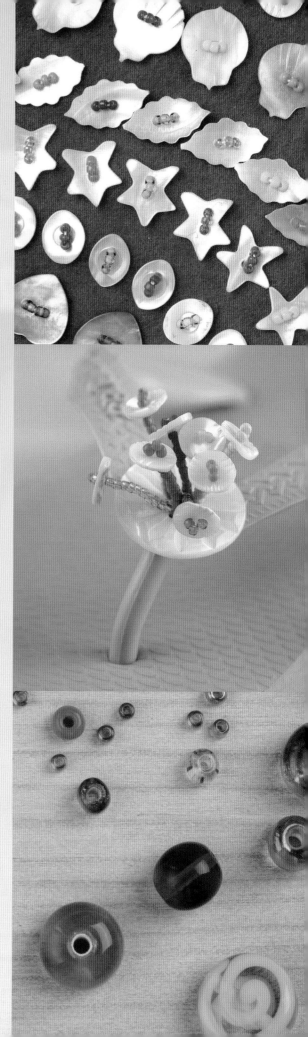

Bevy of Buttons Handbag

Give new life to an old pair of denims with this bright design. Bring the handbag wherever you go, but be prepared for questions—people will be dying to know how they can get their hands on one of these handbags, too!

Materials

Old pair of denims
Sketching supplies
100 round 4-hole buttons, ½" to 1" (1.3 cm to 2.5 cm) in diameter, various colors
1300 to 1700 seed beads, size 11, various colurs
Sewing thread
Beading thread

Sewing needle
Beading needle
Scissors

Directions

 1 Measure 12" (30 cm) from the bottom of one leg of the denims and use a ruler to draw a straight line parallel to the cuff. Cut along the line. This piece forms the body of the handbag.

 2 Thread the sewing needle with sewing thread, double it and tie both ends together. Turn the denim inside-out and make a make a running stitch along the cut end of the denim. This is the base of the handbag.

1

2

4 Repeat step 3 at the other corner of the base, then turn the handbag right-side out.

3 To widen the base, pinch one corner of it between your fingers and flatten to form a triangle. The seam you sewed in step 2 should run down the middle of the triangle and the base of the triangle should be about 1½" (3.8 cm) long. Make a running stitch along the base.

5 Thread the beading needle with a comfortable length of beading thread, double it and tie both ends together.

6 Draw the thread out through the front of the handbag and string 4 to 10 beads.

3

8 Draw the thread out through an empty hole in the same button, thread 5 to 6 beads, and insert on a diagonal into an empty hole, creating an X of beads.

9 Draw the thread back through the first 4 to 10 beads, and back into the denim. Pull gently to secure.

10 Repeat steps 6 to 9, altering the number of beads extending from the handbag, and the colors of the beads and the buttons, to decorate one side of the handbag. You can follow a pattern for attaching the buttons, or work in a random design.

7 Draw the thread through a hole in a button, thread 4 to 5 beads, and insert on a diagonal into an empty hole.

 To make the strap, cut a 42" x 3" (107 cm x 8 cm) strip of denim. Fold the strip in half lengthwise so that the side you want showing is facing inward. Make a running stitch along the cut end of the long side of the strap. Turn the denim right-side out and sew up the ends.

 Making a running stitch to sew each end of the strap onto a seam along the inside of the handbag.

OPTION

This design includes a handmade denim strap, but you can substitute with a ready-made strap or sturdy ribbon. Choose a color that emphasizes the colorful buttons.

Bright Button Lampshade

This art deco lampshade is a perfect accessory for any living room or bedroom. It makes a great housewarming gift, although you may be so pleased with the results, you decide to keep it for yourself!

Materials

Lampshade frame, 4" × 4" × 6" (10 cm × 10 cm × 15 cm)
200 round 4-hole buttons, ½" to ¾" (1.3 cm to 19 cm) in diameter, various colors
250 open jump rings, ½" (1.3 cm) in diameter

Flat-nose pliers
Round-nose pliers

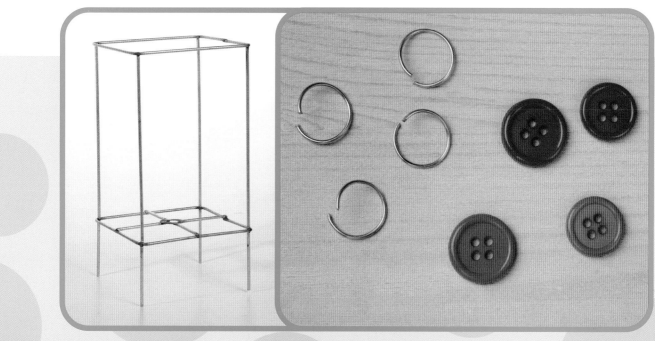

Directions

 Using the pliers, open a jump ring (page 9). Insert each end of the ring into a button and close the ring.

 Open another jump ring and insert one side into the right hole of the button on the right. Insert the other side of the jump ring into another button. Close the jump ring. Continue connecting buttons in this manner until you have a chain of five buttons.

 Repeat steps 1 and 2 to make 32 chains, each of which has five buttons.

 To connect the chains of buttons into panels, line up two button chains, one above the other, on your work surface. Open a jump ring and insert one end in the bottom hole of the leftmost button on the top chain. Insert the other end of the ring in the top hole of the leftmost button on the bottom chain. Repeat along the chain, connecting each button to the button directly below it.

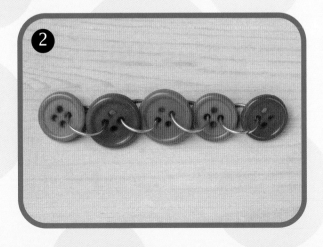

Repeat step 4 to connect eight chains of buttons.

 Repeat steps 4 and 5 to make all four panels.

 To secure a panel to the frame, open a jump ring and insert one end into the top hole of the top leftmost button on the panel. Draw the other end of the ring around the top bar in the frame, at the left side, and close the jump ring. Secure the other five buttons at the top of the panel in the same manner. Do not secure the sides of the panel at this time.

 Repeat step 7 to secure the other panels along the top bars in the frame.

 Once all 4 panels are hanging from the top bar, secure the panels along their sides by attaching them to each other, and to the frame. To do this, open a jump ring and insert one end into the top leftmost button of one of the panels. Draw the other end of the ring around the vertical bar in the frame and through the right hole of the top rightmost button on the adjacent panel. Close the jump ring. Repeat along the length of the panel to secure around the frame and the adjacent panel. Repeat along the edges of all four panels. Secure the bottoms of the panels to the bottom bar in the same manner that you secured the tops of the panels.

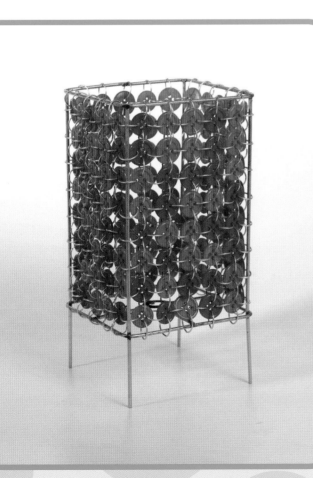

Anything-but-a-Wallflower Sconce

The beauty in this sconce is in its buttons—delicately carved white shell buttons—making it perfect for an elegant living room. Use colorful buttons for a children's bedroom or wooden buttons for a family room or study. This sconce is made of thick paper, but you can also use one made of fabric.

Materials

Cone-shaped paper wall sconce
70 to 100 round white 2-hole shell buttons, ¾" (1.9 cm) in diameter
840 to 1200 seed beads, size 8, silver
Beading thread

Scissors
Beading needle

Directions

1 Thread the needle with a comfortable length of thread, double it and tie both ends together.

2 Insert the thread into the sconce and pull through so that it comes out on the front. Thread 8 beads, then draw the needle through one of the holes in a button.

3 Thread 3 to 4 beads then insert the thread through the other hole. Draw the thread back through the 8 beads and insert into the sconce, close to the point where it was originally drawn out.

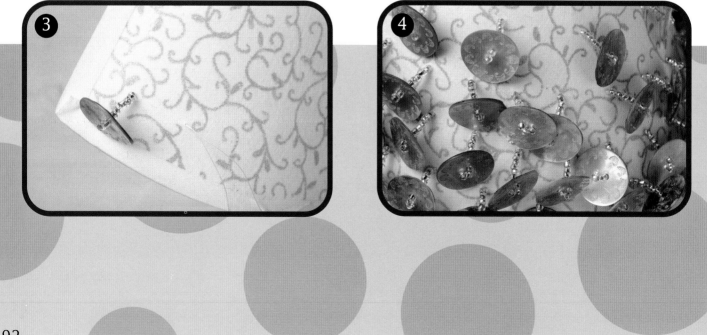

4 Repeat steps 2 and 3 to decorate the front of the sconce with beads and buttons. You can follow a pattern for attaching the buttons, or work in a random design.

OPTION

If you are working with a patterned or decorated sconce, you may want to leave some of the paper showing. Otherwise, feel free to cover the whole sconce with buttons.

Button Up Belt

Transform a simple belt into a stylish accessory with this easy design. You can make this belt from scratch using a synthetic, cotton, or leather strap, or revive an old belt that has been hanging in your closet for years.

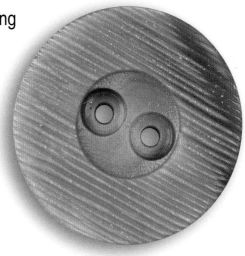

Materials

Sturdy synthetic strap, 1½" × 42" (3.8 cm × 107 cm)
Round belt buckle, 3" (8 cm) in diameter
60 to 80 round buttons, various sizes and colors
180 to 400 seed beads, size 11, various colors
Beading thread

Lighter
Beading needle
Scissors
Punch pliers

Directions

 Measure the strap against your waist (or hips), add another 6" to 8" (15 cm to 20 cm) to one end, and trim. Melt the ends to keep them from fraying.

 Select the hole on your punch pliers that is large enough for the prong on your buckle and punch a hole 2" (5 cm) from one end of the strap.

 Draw the strap through the buckle and insert the prong into the hole. Wrap the strap around the bar in the buckle and make a straight stitch to secure.

 Punch 6 holes at the other end of the strap, each about 1" (2.5 cm) away from the other.

Begin working from the end of the strap with the buckle by sewing a button onto the strap (page 9).

 Draw the thread out the front of the button and string 3 to 5 beads. If it is a 2-hole button, insert the thread into the other hole, and draw through the strap. If it is a 4-hole button, string 4 to 5 beads and insert the thread on a diagonal into the strap. Draw the thread out through an unused hole, string 5 to 6 buttons, and insert on a diagonal into the strap.

 Push the thread out about ½" (1.3 cm) from the edge of the first button. Sew the button onto the strap, then string beads onto the button as described in step 6.

 Repeat step 7 to cover the belt with buttons. Stop about 1½" (3.8 cm) before you reach the series of holes you punched in step 4, so that the buckle fits flatly onto the strap.

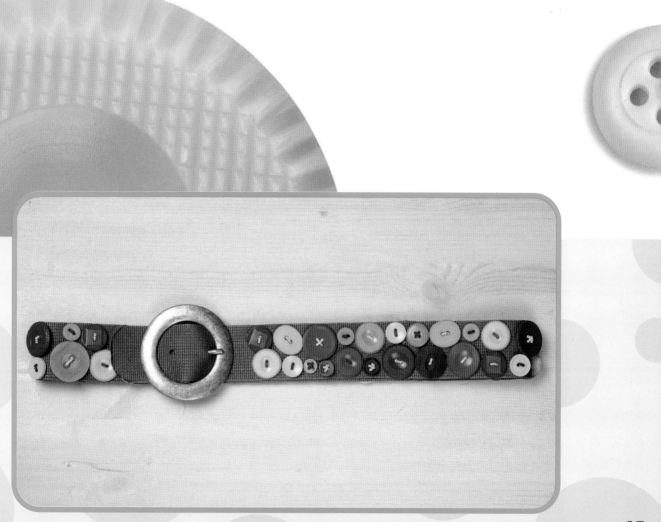

Funky Flip-Flops

With these flip-flops on your feet, your toes will feel fashionably free, and totally funky!

Materials

Pair of flip-flops
2 round white 4-hole shell buttons, 1½" (3.8 cm) in diameter
16 round white 2-hole shell buttons, ¼" (0.6 cm) in diameter
120 seed beads, size 11, various colors
Beading thread

Beading needle
Scissors

To make a stem of beads, draw the thread up through one of the holes in the large button. String 12 beads, then draw the thread through a hole in a small button. String 3 beads then insert the thread into the other hole in the small button. Draw the thread back through the 12 beads, and into the same hole in the large button. Pull gently to secure.

Draw the thread out one of the other holes in the large button and repeat step 3, using a different color of beads, to make another stem.

Directions

Repeat step 4 until each of the holes in the large button has two stems of beads bursting out of it, for a total of eight stems.

Thread the needle with a comfortable length of thread and double it. There is no need to tie the ends together.

Insert the thread in a hole in the large button, draw it over the top of the button and insert on a diagonal into another hole. Pull the thread until there a 2" (5 cm) tail, then tie the thread and tail in a double knot on the underside of the button. Do not cut the tail.

 6 Draw the thread out the underside of the button and tie in a knot with the tail. Cut both ends of the thread close to the knot.

 7 Repeat steps 1 to 6 to make the second button flower.

 8 Thread the needle with comfortable length of thread and double it. There is no need to tie the ends together. Insert the thread in a hole in the button flower, draw it over the top of the button and through another hole. Gently pull the thread until there is a 2" (5 cm) tail.

 9 Place the button flower over the V in the flip-flop strap, at the point where the plastic bar passes between the toes. Tie the tail and the thread in a double knot under the strap, securing the flower button in place. Wrap the thread around the strap a few times, on both sides of the strap and the bar, to secure in place.

 10 Repeat steps 8 and 9 to secure the second button flower onto the second flip-flop.

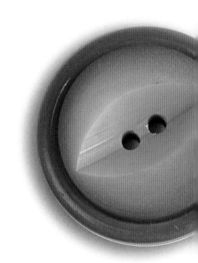

Picture
Perfect Album

With this beautiful album cover, you'll have as much fun looking at the album as you have flipping through the photographs inside!

Materials

Photo album, 7" × 5" × 2" (18 cm × 13 cm × 5 cm)
Sketching supplies
Piece of pink felt, 11" × 16" (28 cm × 41 cm)
110 white 2-hole shell buttons, various shapes and sizes
350 to 500 seed beads, size 11, various colors
Beading thread
2 pieces colorful fabric, 5" × 4" (13 cm × 10 cm)

Scissors
Beading needle
Super glue

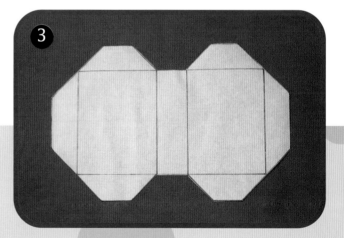

Directions

1 Trace the dimensions of the photo album on a large sheet of paper, making sure to include the front and back covers, and the spine of the album.

2 Add 2" (5 cm) flaps along the edges of the front and back covers of the album. The tops of the flaps can be shorter than the bottoms, so remove a triangular shape from each end, cutting the corners at an angle. Cut out the pattern.

3 Place the pattern on the felt and trace. I suggest using a ruler to make sure the lines are straight.

4 Remove the paper pattern, but don't discard, as you'll need it again in step 5. Cut the felt along the outline.

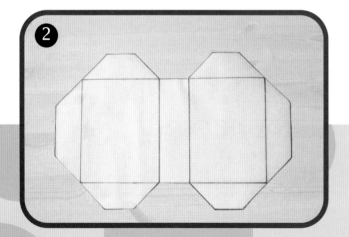

 5 Returning to the paper pattern, cut off the flaps and cut along the lines separating the spine from the front and back covers. Place the patterns for the covers onto the cut felt and trace, using a ruler to make sure the lines are straight. You may also want to sketch a basic pattern for your button design on this side of the felt, to guide you as you work.

 6 Thread the needle with a comfortable length of thread and double it. There is no need to tie the ends together. Turn over the felt so that the front is facing upward and sew on a button (page 9).

 7 Push the thread out the front of one button hole and string 3 to 5 beads. Insert the thread through the other hole and back into the felt.

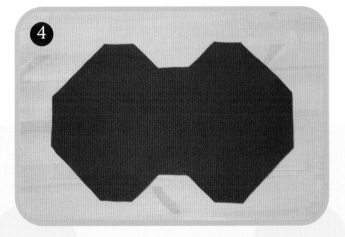

4

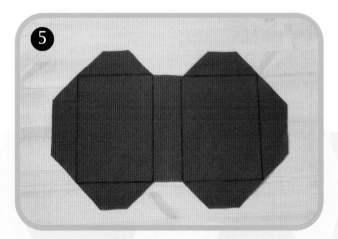

5

Consult your pattern, if necessary, and push the thread out at the spot where you want to secure the next button. First sew the button in place, then draw the thread out again through the first hole, string 3 to 5 beads, and insert into the other hole. Draw the thread out through the back of the felt.

Repeat step 9 until all of the buttons are in place. Take care not to sew any buttons on the flaps of the album cover.

Repeat step 9 until all of the buttons are in place. Take care not to sew any buttons on the album cover flaps.

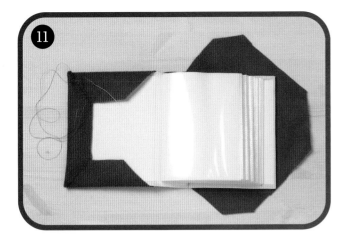

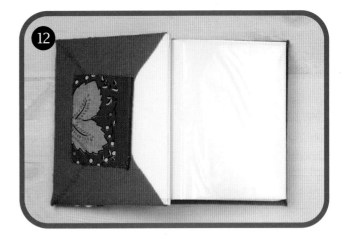

11 To secure the flaps, place dabs of glue on each flap and fold over. Alternately, you can sew the flaps to each other using a whipstitch.

12 Once the flaps are secure, secure the pieces of fabric onto the insides of the front and back of the album cover. You can do this with a few dabs of glue, or by sewing the fabric onto the felt with a whipstitch.

Flowery Hairclip

This flowery hairclip is easy to make, and fun to wear. This design has three flowers, but you can use smaller circles (or a larger barrette) to add even more flowers to the bouquet.

Materials

18 pairs white 2-hole shell buttons, ½" to 1" (1.3 cm to 2.5 cm) in diameter, various shapes
162 pearl beads, ¼" to ½" (0.6 cm to 1.3 cm) in diameter, various colors
180 seed beads, size 11, red
Beading thread
Super glue

Beading needle
Scissors

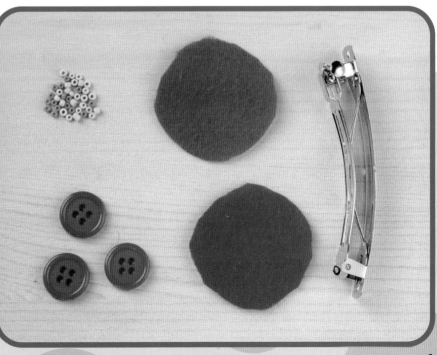

Directions

 Cut each piece of felt into a circle with a 2" (5 cm) diameter. You can use a compass for this, or trace the bottom of a teacup or glass.

 Thread the needle with a comfortable length of thread, double it and tie both ends together.

 Working first with a red circle, insert the needle in the middle of the felt. Sew a running stitch to the edge, then back to the center.

 Gently pull the thread taut to form soft wrinkles in the felt. Tie a knot close to the felt to hold the wrinkles in place.

 Working at a 120° angle from the first row of stitches, make another running stitch from the center of the cloth to the edge, then back to the center.

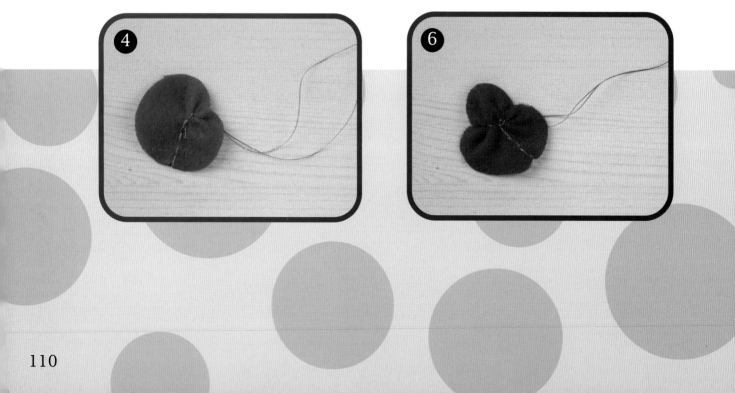

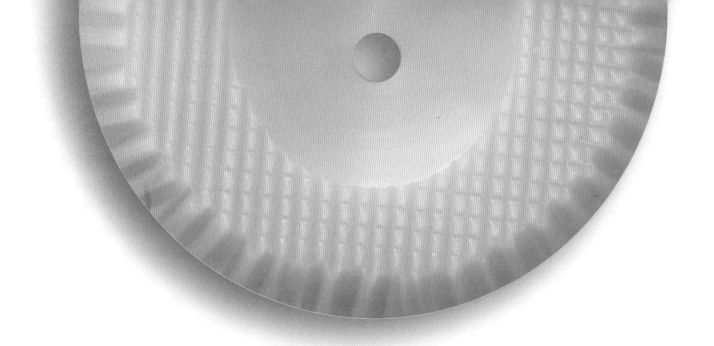

 Gently pull the thread to form soft wrinkles and tie a knot close to the felt to hold the wrinkles in place.

 Repeat steps 5 and 6 to make a third line of stitches. At this point, your felt should have the shape of a three-petal flower.

 Repeat steps 3 to 7 with the other pieces of felt to make 6 three-petal flowers.

 Place a pink flower over a red flower, orienting them so that all 6 petals are showing. Sew the flowers together at the center.

 Repeat step 9 to make two more 6-petal flowers. You can make the flowers identical, or place a pink flower over a red flower, for variety. If you choose this option, be sure to place the different flower in the middle of your hairclip in step 14.

 Working with one flower at a time, sew a button securely onto the center of the flower (page 9).

 Push the thread out the front of one hole in the button and string 3 to 4 beads. Insert the thread back into the button on a diagonal and through the felt. Push out one of the unused holes in the button.

 String 4 to 5 beads, then insert the thread back into the button on a diagonal. Insert the thread into the flower to secure, then tie a double knot and cut the thread close to the knot.

 Repeat 11 to 13 to add buttons to the other flowers. Affix all three flowers to the barrette with a dab or two of glue.